DECLARATION

•

I hereby declare that
all the paper produced
by Cartiere del Garda S.p.A.
in its Riva del Garda mill
is manufactured completely
Acid-free and Wood-free

Dr. Alois Lueftinger
Managing Director and General Manager
Cartiere del Garda S.p.A.

GREEN WORLD

GRASSES AND GRAINS

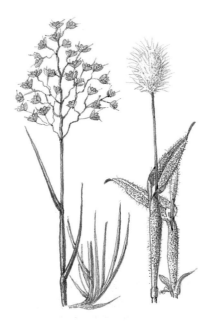

Written by
Theresa Greenaway

STECK-VAUGHN
LIBRARY
A Division of Steck-Vaughn Company
Austin, Texas

**Published in the United States in 1990
by Steck-Vaughn, Co., Austin, Texas,**
a subsidiary of National Education Corporation

A Templar Book
Devised and produced by The Templar Company plc
Pippbrook Mill, London Road, Dorking, Surrey RH4 1JE, Great Britain
Copyright © 1990 by The Templar Company plc

Editor: Wendy Madgwick
Designer: Jane Hunt
Illustrator: Joyce Tuhill

Notes to Reader
There are some words in this book that are printed in **bold** type.
A brief explanation of these words is given in the glossary on p. 44.

All living things are given two Latin names when first classified by a
scientist. Some of them also have a common name, for example meadow
grass, *Poa pratensis*. In this book the common name is used where possible,
but the scientific name is given when first mentioned.

Library of Congress Cataloging-in-Publication Data
Greenaway, Theresa, 1947–
Grasses & grains / by Theresa Greenaway.   p. cm. – (The Green World)
"A Templar Book" – T.p. verso.   Includes bibliographical references.
Summary: Discusses the characteristics of different kinds of grasslands in the
world and describes the structure of grasses, how they grow and develop, the
grains they produce, and their importance to animals and humans.
ISBN 0-8114-2729-3
1. Grasses – Juvenile literature.   2. Grain – Juvenile literature.
3. Grasslands – Juvenile literature.
[1. Grasses.   2. Grasslands.   3. Grains.]
I. Title.   II. Title: Grasses and grains.   III. Series.
QK495.G74G745   1990   90-9563
584'.9–dc20   CIP AC

Color separations by Positive Colour Ltd, Maldon, Essex, Great Britain
Printed and bound by L.E.G.O., Vicenza, Italy
1 2 3 4 5 6 7 8 9 0 LE 94 93 92 91 90

Photographic credits
t = top, b = bottom, l = left, r = right
Cover: Bruce Coleman; page 9 Frank Lane/Holt Studios;
page 11*t* Bruce Coleman/Jeff Foot; page 11*b* Frank Lane/Holt Studios;
page 13 Bruce Coleman/Jeff Foot; page 17 Frank Lane/Phillip Perry; page 21
Frank Lane/A. Wharton; page 25 Spectrum; page 27 Frank Lane/Silvestris;
page 28 Bruce Coleman/Dieter and Mary Plage; page 30 Bruce Coleman/
Lee Lyon; page 31 Bruce Coleman/Gunter Ziesler; page 32 Bruce Coleman/
L.C. Marigo; page 33 Bruce Coleman/J. Cancalosi; page 34 Bruce Coleman/
Leonard Lee Rue III; page 35 ICI Agrochemicals; page 36 Frank Lane/
A. Parker; page 40 ICI Agrochemicals; page 41*t* ICI Agrochemicals;
page 41*b* ICCE/Philip Steele.

CONTENTS

GREEN WORLD

This tree shows the different groups of plants that are found in the world. It does not show how they developed or their relationship with each other.

MONOCOTYLEDONS

- 1 seed leaf or cotyledon
- Leaves with parallel veins

MANY WATER PLANTS
e.g. flowering rush

PALMS e.g. coconut

Lilies, orchids, bananas, rushes, sedges

CONIFEROUS (OR FIR) TREES (Gymnosperms)

FLOWERING PLANTS (Angiosperms)

DICOTYLEDONS

GRASSES
- Two rows of leaves
- Each leaf is long and narrow with a sheath and blade
- Flowers enclosed in paperlike glume

FERNS, CLUB MOSSES AND HORSETAILS (Pteridophytes)

MOSSES AND LIVERWORTS (Bryophytes)

GREEN PLANTS

Group 1
- Woody and "weedy" grasses
- Leaves have square-net veins

ALGAE

PLANTS

Group 2
- Cereals and fodder grasses
- Typical grasses with large seeds

Group 3
- Tropical grasses
- Found in shady forests
- Broad leaves

ANIMALS

FUNGI AND LICHENS

Group 4
- Reeds and pampas grasses

Group 5
- Spinifex, grama grasses, cord grass, and teff
- Grasses of dry regions
- Rolled up leaf blades

BACTERIA

SLIME MOLDS

Group 6
- Spikelets have two flowers
- Sometimes have solid stems

LIVING THINGS

The land area of the world is divided into ten main zones depending on the plants that grow there. The only places that grasses cannot grow are in the frozen Antarctic and in the salt oceans.

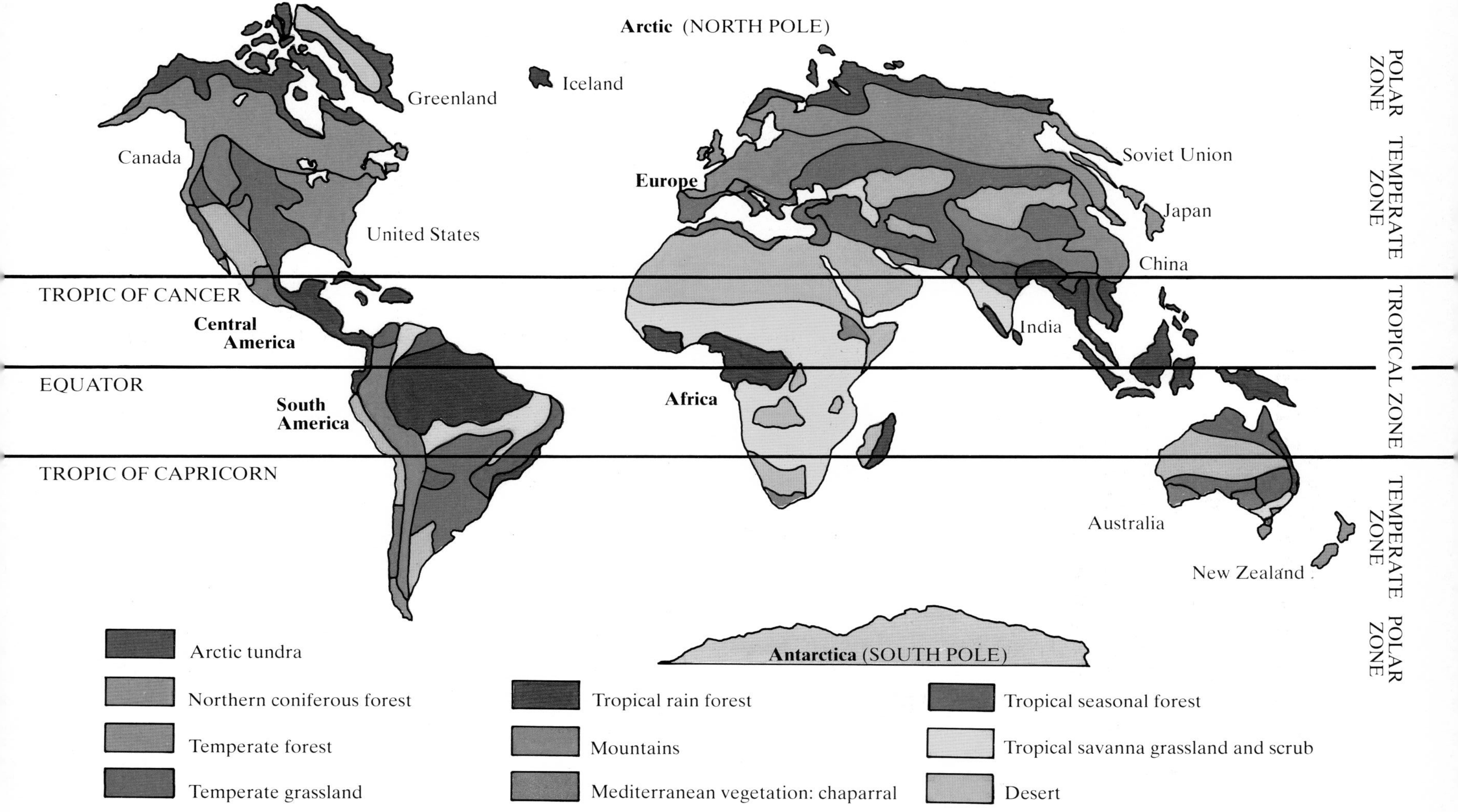

| POLAR ZONE | TEMPERATE ZONE | TROPICAL ZONE | TEMPERATE ZONE | POLAR ZONE |

TROPIC OF CANCER

EQUATOR

TROPIC OF CAPRICORN

Arctic (NORTH POLE)

Iceland

Greenland

Canada

United States

Central America

South America

Soviet Union

Japan

China

India

Europe

Africa

Australia

New Zealand

Antarctica (SOUTH POLE)

Arctic tundra

Northern coniferous forest

Temperate forest

Temperate grassland

Tropical rain forest

Mountains

Mediterranean vegetation: chaparral

Tropical seasonal forest

Tropical savanna grassland and scrub

Desert

GRASSES

Grasses are green plants that belong to the group called **angiosperms** (meaning covered seeds) or flowering plants. They have flowers that produce male cells protected in **pollen grains**, and female cells (**ovules**, see p. 18). When these cells fuse or join, a **seed** is produced which will grow into the new plant. This seed grows inside a **fruit** (see p. 20) which protects it. Flowering plants are divided into two main groups, **dicotyledons**, which have two first leaves or cotyledons inside the seed, and **monocotyledons**, which have only one. All grasses are monocotyledons.

The grass family is the fifth largest with about 8,000 kinds or species. They all have long, narrow leaves, upright stems, and threadlike roots. Some are less than an inch high, but others grow to three feet or more – one bamboo can grow to 100 feet.

Types of grasses

Grasses come in all shapes and sizes but they all rely on the wind to blow the pollen grains from one flower to another. They have small, dull flowers and the petals do not produce nectar, a sweet, sugary solution, or scent. The flowers produce large amounts of light, powdery pollen which is easily carried by the wind.

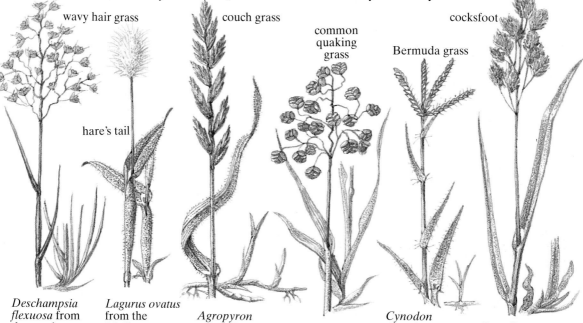

wavy hair grass

couch grass

cocksfoot

common quaking grass

Bermuda grass

hare's tail

Deschampsia flexuosa from the northeast U.S., Europe, northern Asia, and temperate South America

Lagurus ovatus from the Mediterranean, is now in the U.S., Australia, South America, and South Africa

Agropyron repens from Europe and temperate Asia, is now in temperate countries

Briza media from Europe and north and west Asia

Cynodon dactylon from the U.S., South Africa, India, and Australia, now in Europe

Dactylis glomerata from Europe, North Africa, and temperate Asia

Feeding the world

The chief importance of grasses is that they provide food for both people and animals. Many of the world's animals from tiny mice to majestic elephants graze upon grasses, and numerous small birds and animals eat grass seed. These grass-eating animals, in turn, provide food for meat-eating animals and birds.

People cannot eat the grass plant. Most of the world's people depend on the seed or grain of a group of grasses known as cereals.

Binding the soil

Grasses are good for the soil, too. Their dense network of roots binds together the soil surface and prevents soil erosion, which is when bare soil is blown or washed away. Grasses also help to make soil fertile as dead plants and insects become caught in the grass rootlets. This increases the fertility of sandy soils and helps them to hold moisture. Clay soils are heavy and wet. The fine fibrous rootlets prevent the clay from sticking in lumps, and improve drainage.

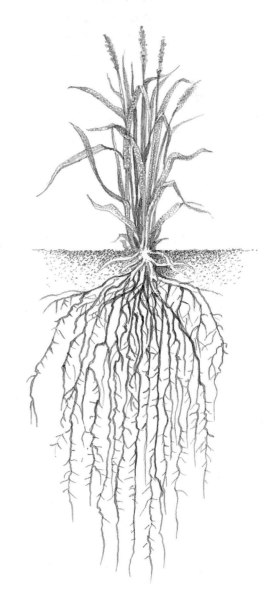

■ Grasses contain the green pigment **chlorophyll**. They use this to make their own food from water and carbon dioxide, a gas, using the energy of sunlight. This is called **photosynthesis**.
■ They are flowering plants or angiosperms.
■ They have small wind-pollinated flowers without showy petals, scent, or nectar.
■ They are monocotyledons.
■ They include food cereals for humans and for grazing cattle.
■ Grasses are found everywhere except in the ice-covered poles and in very dry deserts.

WORLD GRASSLANDS

Rainfall and temperature together make up the climate of a region. For instance, it may be hot and wet, or cold and wet. Climate controls the kinds of plants or vegetation that can grow in each region. On the basis of this natural vegetation, the land area of the world is divided into ten large zones (see the map on p. 7). A zone and the animals that live in it is known as a biome. Although these zones are natural regions, each one has been altered by human activities.

There are two grassland zones. One, the savanna, is found in the hotter parts of the world, between the Tropics of Cancer and Capricorn. It covers about 15 percent of the world's land surface. The largest area of natural savanna is in tropical Africa. Smaller areas are found in South America, India, and Australia.

The second zone is the temperate grassland. It covers about 12 percent of the world's land surface, and occurs in all the continents except for frozen Antarctica.

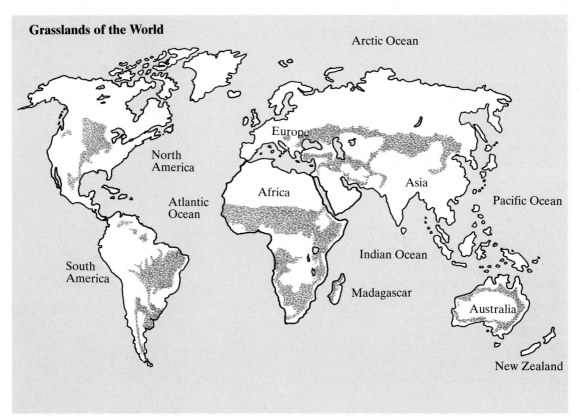

Grasslands of the World

Arctic Ocean

Europe

North America

Asia

Atlantic Ocean

Africa

Pacific Ocean

South America

Indian Ocean

Madagascar

Australia

New Zealand

Climate

Savanna grassland, like this African savanna, is warm all year round, with no real winter. In the "summer," with average temperatures of 85°F, savannas are among the hottest places on Earth. Few trees grow in this hot grassland.

The annual rainfall of the savanna may be as much as 60 inches, but it all falls during 2 to 3 months known as the wet season. Grasses and other plants grow and flower, and the few trees put out new leaves. In the long dry season, no rain falls and the ground becomes parched.

Temperate grasslands have hot summers and cold winters. The ground freezes and there may be harsh winds. The annual rainfall is lower than in savannas, but it falls more evenly throughout the year. Even so, with only between 10 and 30 inches a year, some areas are quite dry. Rain that falls in the summer often dries up quickly from the warm ground.

Soils

The soils of the tropical savannas are not all the same. Some are poor and infertile, lacking in nutrients. Where there are more fertile soils, and the rainfall is not too low, more trees may grow, as well as the tall savanna grasses.

The soils of the temperate grasslands, like the one shown here, are often very good. They have mineral nutrients and are rich in humus or plant and animal remains. This rich, deep earth has a dark topsoil called chernozem. In spite of this, few trees grow because the climate is too dry. These grasslands are very fertile and are used as farmland.

STEPPES AND PRAIRIES

The largest area of natural temperate grassland is the steppe. It is about 954,000 square miles in area, stretching from Hungary and Austria in the west, across the Soviet Union to Mongolia and China in the east. Originally these flat, lowland plains were huge areas of short grasses where herds of wild animals roamed.

Most of the steppe has been plowed up and planted to feed the large population of the Soviet Union. Wheat is the most important crop, but oats, corn, barley, and rye are also grown. Non-cereal crops include potatoes, flax, sugar beet, and vegetables.

In the central lowlands of North America lie the great plains and prairies of the U.S. and Canada.

They stretch from the foothills of the Rockies in the west to the forests along the east of North America. The rainfall is higher in the eastern prairies, so that trees can grow, especially along the river valleys.

The early pioneers of European descent hunted the bison, which grazed the grasslands, to near extinction and put sheep and cattle to graze in their place. They plowed up the tough prairie turf and planted grains, cotton, potatoes, and other food crops. The native plants and animals were squeezed into smaller and smaller patches of land.

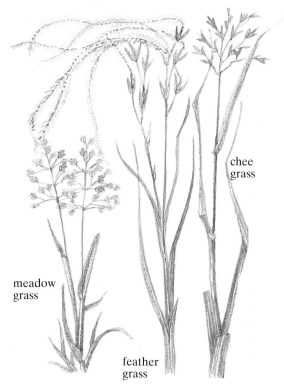

chee grass

meadow grass

feather grass

Grasses and animals of the steppe

Meadow grass (*Poa pratensis*) is a common grass of the steppe. This grass and some fescues (*Festuca* species) provided food for the herds of animals that used to live there. Feather grass (*Stipa pennata*) has flowers with feathery parts called **awns** about 12 inches long at their tips. On the drier steppe, tussocks of chee grass (*Stipa splendens*) are found. This drought-resistant grass has tough flower stems six feet tall.

The natural grazers of the steppe grasslands were the saiga antelopes, the onager (wild ass), and wild horses. They lived in herds, moving from place to place. At ground level, animals such as sousliks (ground squirrels) and gerbils fed on the roots, leaves, and seeds of grasses.

Animals of the prairies

Huge herds of bison and pronghorn antelope, the natural grazers of the prairies, used to roam the land, but both were overhunted. By 1890 over 50 million bison had been killed and fewer than 1,000 remained. Similarly, the number of pronghorns had been reduced from about 35 million to 13,000 by the 1920s. Today both animals are protected, and there are over 50,000 bison and 500,000 pronghorns.

Grasses of the prairies

Before the prairies were plowed up, big bluestem (*Andropogon gerardii*) was the most common grass, covering large areas. Although a good pasture grass, it is now rare in many places. Needlegrasses, switchgrass, and Indian grass are all tall prairie grasses with flowerstems five to eight feet tall. Shorter grasses grow on the drier plains to the west. Blue grama grass (*Bouteloua gracilis*), buffalo grass (*Buchloe dactyloides*), and wheatgrass (*Agropyron smithii*) are the most abundant. Less than six feet tall, these are all good grasses for grazing animals.

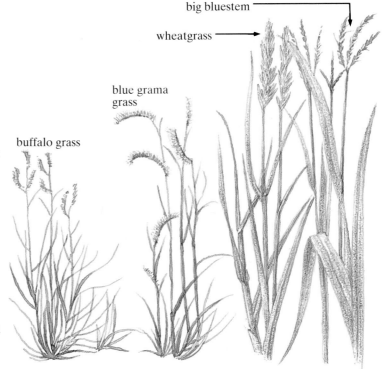

big bluestem

wheatgrass

blue grama grass

buffalo grass

THE PAMPAS AND VELD

The pampas, another temperate grassland, is a fertile plain in the middle of Argentina, in South America. Like all great plains, it is sometimes swept by strong winds. Before the Spanish settlers arrived in the sixteenth century, the pampas was covered with grasses and an occasional tree. Today, it is no longer a wild place. Fruit, corn, and vegetables are grown on the parts of the pampas with the most rain, and wheat is grown in the drier places.

Sheep and cattle are grazed on grassland that cannot be used to grow wheat.

The veld covers most of South Africa. The many kinds of animals – antelopes, gazelles, elephants, lions – that once made their home there are now confined to game reserves and national parks. Large flocks of sheep graze in their place. The areas with more plentiful rains are rich in fertile lands where fruit and vegetables such as corn are grown.

Grasses of the pampas

Pampas grasses grow in large, thick tussocks. The most common is *Cortaderia selloana*, which has male and female flowers on separate plants. The female flowerhead is a silvery, silky plume up to 3 feet long. On damper parts of the pampas, especially near rivers, uva grass (*Gynerium sagittatum*) grows – it can be 30 feet tall!

Feeding and Food-Chains

Grasses are often dry and stiff and animals and insects need strong jaws to chew them. Grasshoppers and locusts have tough, horny lower jaws or mandibles. Rodents and larger grazing animals have sharp front teeth to cut off the grass and big, grinding back teeth.

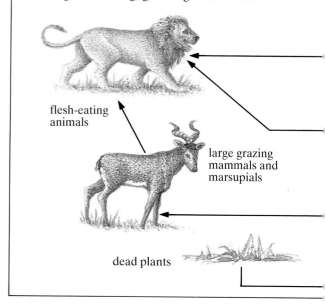

flesh-eating animals

large grazing mammals and marsupials

dead plants

Australia's temperate grasslands

These are in the lowlands of southern Australia. Among the scattered eucalyptus trees, Mitchell grasses (*Astrebla* species) grow on the drier areas. Millets, couch, and paspalum grasses grow on damper ground near rivers.

Kangaroos and wallabys are the natural grazers of Australia's grasslands. They once traveled freely over the land, feeding wherever there was fresh, green grass. Sheep and cattle are now grazed on the better grasslands, and the kangaroos are fenced out.

Mitchell grasses

Insects are an important link in the grassland food-chain or ecosystem. They feed on the tough grasses and then birds, reptiles, and animals feed on the insects' much softer bodies. Sometimes, locusts reproduce too much, causing enormous swarms to form. They can do great damage by eating crops.

When plants and animals die, their bodies are broken down or decayed by other **organisms** (living things) like fungi and bacteria. The feces or dung of the animals are also broken down. The nutrients that plants need to grow are returned to the soil and the cycle starts again.

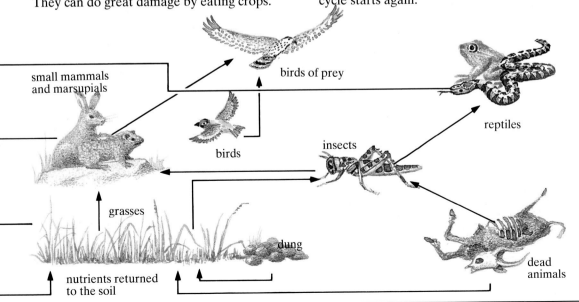

small mammals and marsupials

birds of prey

reptiles

birds

insects

grasses

dung

dead animals

nutrients returned to the soil

15

SAVANNAS

Africa has the largest area of tropical savanna. There are smaller savanna grasslands and savanna forests in other tropical places such as the West Indies, South America, India, and Australia.

Africa's savannas are open, empty tracts of land. There are a few spiny, flat-topped *Acacia* trees which can survive the long dry season. In the wetter parts, small groves of trees may flourish. In the drier regions there are no trees at all. Here, even the grasses are reduced to scattered clumps.

Many of the African big game animals like zebra and wildebeest graze together in herds of up to 10,000 animals. Others, such as the white rhinoceros and the elephant, are seriously threatened mostly from poaching. Native animals rarely graze an area too much, but the savanna is under threat from cattle.

Grasses of the African savanna

Elephant grass (*Pennisetum purpureum*) is a widespread grass that grows to 16 feet. Its stiff leaves tangle with the lower branches of trees in places, making a dense undergrowth. Rooigrass (*Themeda triandra*), *Andropogon*, *Hyparrhenia*, and *Cymbopogon* are all tall grasses common on the savanna. *Sporobolus marginatus* and *Chloris pycnothrix* are two favorite fodder grasses of wild animals.

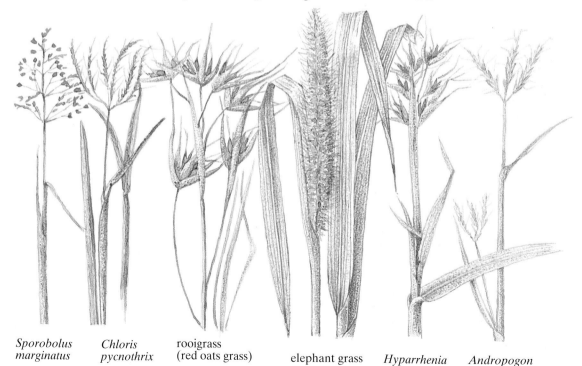

Sporobolus marginatus   *Chloris pycnothrix*   rooigrass (red oats grass)   elephant grass   *Hyparrhenia*   *Andropogon*

Savanna forests

In the savanna forests of Southeast Asia, a dry season is followed by 6 months of monsoon rains. During the monsoon a forest of deciduous trees flourishes. On the forest floor, there is a dense growth of pygmy bamboos, other grasses, and broad-leaved plants. The trees shed their leaves in the dry season. The people of these forests regularly set fire to them, burning dead leaves and bamboo stems. When the rains return, trees, bamboos, and other grasses spring back to life.

Bamboos

Bamboos grow in monsoon savanna forests and tropical and temperate rain forests. They are the most primitive grasses. There are about 832 species. They range from small, slender plants to the giant *Dendrocalamus giganteus* which can grow 115 feet tall. Most are found in Asia, Central and South America, and Africa. They flourish on tropical riverbanks and on the slopes of the Andes and Himalayas.

Unlike other grasses, bamboos have woody stems that branch near the top. Most of the leaf-blades are on these branches, so the taller bamboos look like trees. Their flowers are typical grass flowers which open in clusters at the tips of the branches. Some flower every year, just like other grasses, but others flower far less often, maybe only once every 20 to 120 years! Bamboos of the same kind all flower together and after flowering, they die.

The giant panda, one of the world's rarest animals, feeds on bamboo. They live in cool rain forests of the Szechuan and Shensi provinces of western China. Beneath the conifer and broad-leaved evergreen trees are jungles of bamboos. Pandas feed mainly on *Sinarundinaria* bamboos, which grow up to 13 feet tall. To survive, a panda needs to eat 20 to 45 pounds of bamboo a day.

STRUCTURE OF GRASSES

Like all flowering plants, grasses are made up of roots, stems, flowers, and leaves. They all follow a general pattern, but each species differs in detail and is unique. The general structure of a grass can be seen by looking at the diagram opposite. Both the green stem and the leaves, which are long and thin, are used to make food (see p. 22).

The flowers of grasses have the same basic structure as all flowering plants. The male **stamens** are made up of a **filament**, or stalk, and a head, the **anther**, which produces the male pollen grains. The female part, the **carpel**, is made up of the **ovary** (which contains the ovule) and a stalk or **style** with a **stigma** at the top.

The pollen is transferred from the anther of one plant to the stigma of another by the wind. The petals are therefore very small so that they do not shield the anthers and stigmas. The mature anthers and stigmas hang down outside the flower so that the pollen can be blown away by the wind or picked up from it. Each flower stem bears a group of flowers as a flowerhead or inflorescence. Grasses can be easily identified by looking at their flowerheads.

Flowerheads

The flowerhead is either an unbranched **spike** or a branched **panicle**. On the stem of the spike, or the branches of the panicle, there are groups of flowers, called spikelets. A spikelet may contain many little flowers, or only one. At the base of the spikelet is a pair of green scales or **glumes**, which often bear a stiff spike, an awn, at the tip.

Each little flower is enclosed by a **lemma** and **palea**. Inside these are usually three stamens, a **pistil** (made up of one carpel) and two very tiny scales called **lodicules**. These lodicules are probably all that remain of the petals. The stigmas are often very feathery so that they can trap the pollen.

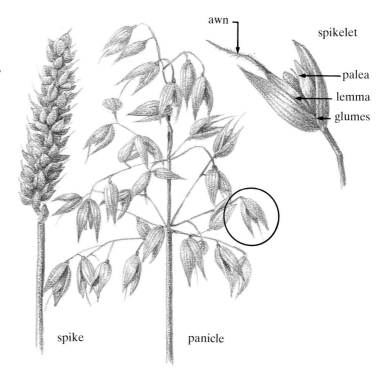

awn

spikelet

palea

lemma

glumes

spike

panicle

The Structure of a Grass

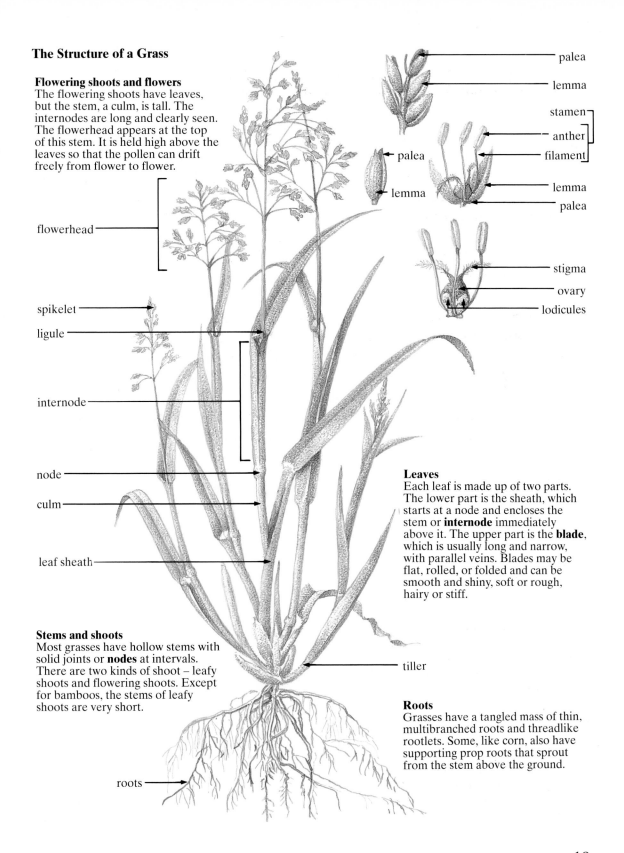

Flowering shoots and flowers
The flowering shoots have leaves, but the stem, a culm, is tall. The internodes are long and clearly seen. The flowerhead appears at the top of this stem. It is held high above the leaves so that the pollen can drift freely from flower to flower.

flowerhead

spikelet

ligule

internode

node

culm

leaf sheath

palea
lemma

palea
lemma

stamen — anther, filament

lemma
palea

stigma
ovary
lodicules

Leaves
Each leaf is made up of two parts. The lower part is the sheath, which starts at a node and encloses the stem or **internode** immediately above it. The upper part is the **blade**, which is usually long and narrow, with parallel veins. Blades may be flat, rolled, or folded and can be smooth and shiny, soft or rough, hairy or stiff.

tiller

Stems and shoots
Most grasses have hollow stems with solid joints or **nodes** at intervals. There are two kinds of shoot – leafy shoots and flowering shoots. Except for bamboos, the stems of leafy shoots are very short.

Roots
Grasses have a tangled mass of thin, multibranched roots and threadlike rootlets. Some, like corn, also have supporting prop roots that sprout from the stem above the ground.

roots

19

FROM FLOWER TO SEED

When the dustlike pollen is released from the anthers, it is wafted away by breezes. Pollination occurs when the pollen lands on a stigma and a pollen tube begins to grow. If a flower is pollinated by pollen from another plant, it is **cross-pollinated**. If it is pollinated by its own pollen, then **self-pollination** has occurred.

Forming seeds
The pollen grain develops a pollen tube which grows down the style into the ovary. The male cell joins with or **fertilizes** the female ovule to form a seed. If the pollen is from another plant, **cross-fertilization** or crossing occurs. If it is from the same plant it is **self-fertilization**. Unlike self-fertilization, crossing produces offspring with different characteristics from the parent plant.

This may mean that they can spread and colonize different areas or habitats.

The seed is made up of two different parts – the **endosperm**, which stores food, and the **embryo**, which will develop into the new plant. The seed is surrounded by a tough coat or **testa**. In grasses, the endosperm is very large. It is this part which is used by people to make flour or cereals.

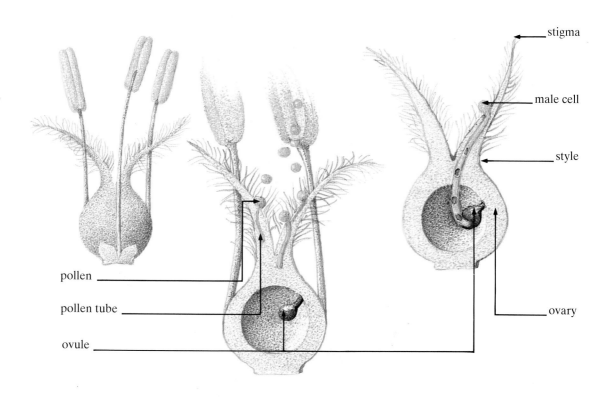

stigma

male cell

style

ovary

pollen

pollen tube

ovule

How grasses spread

By the time the seed is ripe, the flowerhead is brittle and dry. It is time for the seeds to be spread. The dispersal of the seeds ensures that they are spread over a wide area, which helps to avoid overcrowding.

In some tropical grasses, and cultivated wheat, the "seeds" (really the caryopsis) fall freely from the papery bracts. In other species, the grains are shed still tightly enclosed in the papery lemma and palea, or even as a complete spikelet containing one or more seeds. The flowerheads of many grasses break so that each seed unit also has a short, sharp piece of branchlet firmly attached to it.

These small, papery units are light and are readily spread by the wind. They also float and so may be spread by rivers, streams, or even heavy rain water running over the ground. Some grasses have long, bristly awns or little hooks. These seed units stick to the fur and feathers of animals and birds and are spread as the animals move around.

Fruits

The grass fruit is called a **caryopsis**. The fruit wall develops from the ovary, and unlike many other flowering plants, it is very thin and clings closely to the seed inside. Some *Melocanna* bamboos have fleshy pear-shaped berries. The plant and fruit can be used for various purposes.

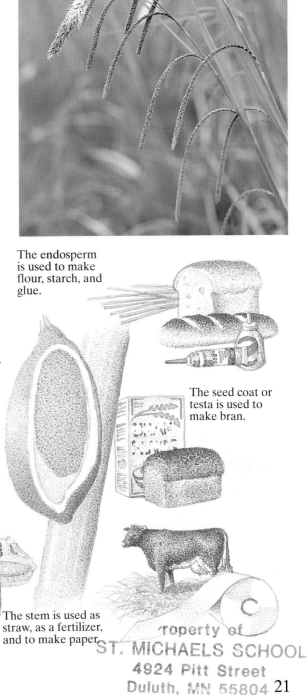

The endosperm is used to make flour, starch, and glue.

The seed coat or testa is used to make bran.

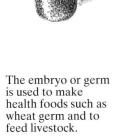

The whole grain is used to make breakfast cereals and beer and whisky.

The embryo or germ is used to make health foods such as wheat germ and to feed livestock.

The stem is used as straw, as a fertilizer, and to make paper.

HOW GRASSES GROW

After the ripe seed has been shed, it does not **germinate** or grow immediately. This interval between seed ripening and germination is called **dormancy**. Dormancy ensures that seeds do not start to grow at the wrong time. Some species have seeds that start to grow very soon after they have been shed. Most do not begin to grow until the spring, or the beginning of the wet season in tropical climates. Not all seeds germinate in the following year. If the ground is too dry, or the seed is buried too deeply, germination is delayed. Different plants vary in the length of time their seeds can remain alive, but dormant. For most grasses and cereals, this is between two and six years.

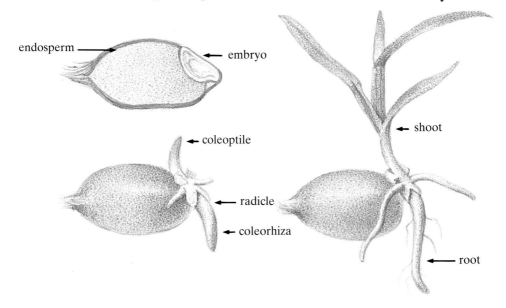

endosperm — embryo
coleoptile
radicle
coleorhiza
shoot
root

Germination

If there is enough moisture, oxygen, and the temperature is right the grass seed swells and the embryo starts to grow using the food stored in the endosperm. First, the radicle, or young root, protected by a sheath called the coleorhiza, develops. The root is attracted by the pull of the Earth's gravity and grows down into the soil. Then the shoot, protected in a coleoptile, emerges. It grows upward toward the light. Gradually the root and shoot systems develop. As each side shoot or tiller grows from the short leafy stems, a tuft of grass takes shape. Once the shoots reach the light, they develop a green pigment, chlorophyll, and begin to make their own food by photosynthesis (see p. 9).

As the buds and growing points of the leaves are close to the ground, they are not eaten by browsing animals. Grazed grass blades quickly regrow, replenishing the food supply. The buds are only nibbled away when too many animals feed off the same land. When this happens, the grass is slow to recover, and the turf is worn away by trampling hooves.

Annuals and perennials

After a phase in which only leafy shoots grow, the flowering shoots appear. For most grasses, this phase lasts a few weeks. For others, it can be longer. Some bamboos have never been known to flower.

The young flowerstem does not make any more new leaves or tillers. Instead, a little flowerhead develops at its tip and the stem grows longer and thinner. Grasses of the same species growing in the same region all flower and fruit together. An annual grass, one that lasts only a year, dies after flowering. A perennial, one that lasts for many years, continues to grow, and flowers again the following year.

annual meadow grass   perennial rye grass

Spreading Without Flowers

In some plants, for example the viviparous fescue (*Festuca vivipara*), the spikelets develop into little plantlets while still attached to the flower stems. When the flower stem dies and rots away, these plantlets drop to the ground and root.

Many grasses grow into a clump or tussock. Others spread to make a mat over the ground. This is achieved by **rhizomes** or **stolons**. A rhizome is an underground stem that grows sideways through the soil. Roots and shoots appear at each node (see p. 19). Stolons are also stems, but these spread over the surface of the ground, sending out shoots and roots at the nodes.

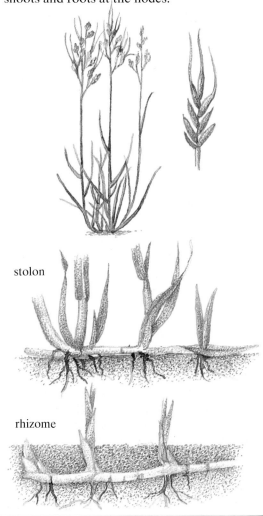

stolon

rhizome

GRASSES OF WET PLACES

Grasses are found throughout the world but different kinds are found in different habitats. For example, those that live in wet areas cannot live in dry places and vice-versa.

Salt marshes are found in quiet, sheltered coastal waters. There are salt marshes on cold arctic coasts and the coasts of warmer, temperate regions. They are all regularly flooded with salt water as the incoming tide quietly fills the creeks and pools. At high tides, water covers the low hummocks of salt marsh vegetation.

Mud and silt settle out from the still waters, and on this the salt marsh plants grow. Plants that live in these salty conditions are called halophytes. Grasses are an important part of salt marsh vegetation. They bind the mud and make a tough mat of stems and leaves. Some are short, for example the common salt marsh grass (*Puccinellia maritima*) is only 4 to 30 inches tall. It is common in northeast American and west European salt marshes. Cord grasses are taller and coarser. They grow in very deep, soft mud.

Freshwater marshes

In freshwater marshes and lakes *Phragmites* reeds grow. These tall, stiff-stemmed grasses can form large reedbeds. They provide shelter, nesting sites, and food for birds and water animals. The reeds are also cut and used for thatching.

Common Cord Grass

Until the nineteenth century, only one species of cord grass – the small cord grass (*Spartina maritima*) – grew on mudflats around the coasts of southern England and Wales. Then, the smooth cord grass (*Spartina alternifolia*) from the U.S. was planted in the U.K. Brought close together, the two species bred with each other and by the 1890s, a new cord grass was spreading rapidly over the mudflats.

Now called the common cord grass (*Spartina anglica*), it has spread over mudflats and salt marshes very quickly by means of thick rhizomes or swollen roots. It also makes fertile seeds. It stabilizes soft mud very rapidly, soon turning a salt marsh into pasture, fit for grazing. It has been planted in other parts of the U.S., U.K., Europe, and Australia.

Unfortunately, native salt marsh plants could not compete and disappeared in many places. Also, by covering these mudflats, the feeding grounds of wading birds were greatly reduced. The spread of this grass into salt marsh communities is being controlled.

small
cord grass

common
cord grass

The Danube delta

The Danube River runs through Rumania to the Black Sea. The largest reedbeds in the world grow in the huge area where the river meets the sea. The river deposits 80 million tons of silt there every year. It is one of the richest of wetlands, teeming with wildlife. Enormous flocks of migrating birds visit the reedbeds and many breed in the dense, floating islands of reeds.

GRASSES OF DRY PLACES

Plants that can live in very dry areas are called xerophytes. They have various ways of conserving water. They have leaves with hard, waxy skins, which roll inward so that each blade is a spiky, narrow tube. This keeps **evaporation** or loss of water as low as possible. They also have very long roots that can reach water deep in the ground. These extremely tough, hard grasses have little food value for animals.

When sand is blown off the beaches, it piles up into dunes 30 to 90 feet high. Marram grasses (*Ammophila* species) bind the shifting sands of coastal dunes.

The sand dune is a difficult place for plants to grow. First, the sand is very unstable. Second, it is very, very dry. Even after a shower, the water drains away quickly. Third, it gets very hot in the sun and cools quickly at night. Finally, sand has little humus and few nutrients. Even when marram grass is very well established, the surface of the sand is still loose.

Atriplex littoralis

Ammophila arenaria

Festuca rubra arenaria

Coastal sand dunes

Marram grass has thick branching rhizomes that spread rapidly through the sand, growing up to 12 inches in 4 weeks. The tall, dense tufts of leaves trap more sand, and the dune builds up on the side nearest the water. If the shoots are buried, they grow up through the sand.

Eventually, a system of dunes and hollows called slacks is formed. The oldest parts of the dunes are those farthest inland. Marram grass dies out as the dunes are colonized by other plants, and fescue grasses (for example the red fescue, *Festuca rubra arenaria*) take over. The older dunes are rich in wild flowers and animals.

1. *Atriplex littoralis* grows on the drift line of a high spring tide.

2. Sand dunes form. *Ammophila arenaria* starts to grow.

3. The sand dunes build up. Marram grasses spread.

4. Dune grows as wind blows sand inland.

5. Marram grasses are replaced by fescue grasses.

6. Older dunes flatten and younger dunes form. Different grasses grow in damp hollows.

Inland sand dunes

Ancient sand dunes and thin sandy or stony soils cover much of northern and central Australia. The rainfall is low and the sun is scorching. Often, the only plants to be seen are spinifex grasses (*Triodia* species). There are about 50 species and they are found only in Australia.

They grow in clumps and their long roots push down to underground water. Shorter feeding roots grow out sideways. As the clump grows outward, the center dies, making a "ring." These grasses are the mainstay of life in this harsh climate. They provide food for insects and birds, which in turn are eaten by other animals.

HUMAN-MADE GRASSLAND

People have felled forests for thousands of years. The timber was used for building houses, boats, and for firewood, and the newly cleared land was used to graze livestock or to plant crops. As the population increased, more and more land was cleared so that in many temperate countries, little remains of the natural covering of woodlands.

Land that has been specially planted with grasses for cattle, sheep, or horses to feed on is called pasture. A meadow is land where this grass is allowed to grow tall and is then cut for hay. Cattle need longer, richer grass than sheep or goats, so, in general, cows are found in fertile lowland pastures. Sheep and goats can thrive on the poorer grasslands of mountain slopes, downs, and moors.

Human-made grasslands in the tropics

Large areas of the once-vast tropical rain forests are being felled every year. The huge tree trunks are taken away and unwanted trees and branches are burned. In some parts of the world, a savanna grassland is then established where beef cattle are reared. Sometimes, crops are planted on the cleared land. However, the topsoil of the rain forests is thin and closely knit by the tree roots. When the forests are cleared, this thin soil is quickly exhausted or eroded by weather or over-grazing. Beneath the topsoil lies an ancient, hard layer called laterite. This is too poor for crops or good grassland, and the rain forest trees cannot regrow either. The areas become barren and useless.

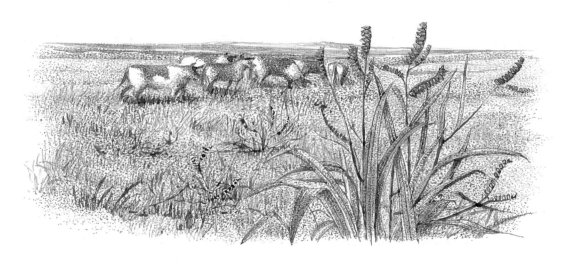

Improvement of tropical pastures

To stop further destruction of rain forests, scientists in Colombia, South America, are trying to improve the poor pastures, called llanos. They have planted three nutritious grasses from tropical Africa (*Brachiaria decumbens,* *B. humidicola*, and *B. dictyonema*) which grow well on poor soils. They cover the ground with a dense turf, which helps to stop soil erosion. When they are sown with plants like clover, which fix nitrogen, they need only small amounts of fertilizers, and beef cattle like to eat them.

A good pasture

Many temperate countries, for example the U.K., New Zealand, and southern Australia, are famous for dairy cattle kept on lush pastures. Although there are nearly 160 species of grass native to temperate regions, the farmer plants only about ten of these. The best pastures are on deep, rich soil. The farmer chooses grasses that are leafy, nutritious, and pleasant for animals to eat. Grasses that start to grow early in spring and continue growing well until late autumn are best. Grasses with many tough stems, or leaves that are rough or hairy are not suitable.

One of the most important pasture grasses is perennial rye-grass (*Lolium perenne*). The value of a pasture is measured by the percentage of this grass it contains. The best pastures have at least 30 percent of this rye-grass, together with others such as timothy (*Phleum pratense)*, cocksfoot grass (*Dactylis glomerata*), and white clover. Plant breeders have bred especially leafy strains of these valuable grasses.

ANIMALS IN GRASSLANDS

The lives of grassland animals are closely linked with the life-cycle of the grasses and the seasons of the year. No matter how many different kinds of animals there are, they all depend on the grasses. In turn, the animals spread the grass seeds and their dung and dead bodies provide nutrients to enrich the soil and enable the grasses to grow.

Before the plains and prairies of North America were turned into farmland, bison herds migrated north in the hot summer to feed on more juicy grasses. In winter, they returned south, avoiding the snow. Similar migrations occur in the African savanna.

Birds of the grassland

Birds form an important part of the grassland ecosystem. They can fly to a good food supply and some regularly migrate thousands of miles. The upland plover, which feeds on seeds and insects, nests on the American prairies as far north as Alaska. In winter, it flies south to the pampas grasslands in Argentina.

The rose-colored starling, a bird of the steppes, feeds on grasshoppers and locusts. They are very welcome in areas where crops are infested with plagues of locusts.

The red-billed quelea, a small weaver bird, roosts in reedbeds of the African savanna. During the day, enormous flocks fly far over the grassland to feed. Although they do eat termites and insects, their main food is grass seed. They prefer the small seeds of wild grasses, but will unfortunately ransack crops such as millet and sorghum when wild seed becomes scarce. Quelea are a serious pest and local farmers try to control the immense numbers. By the end of the dry season, many will have starved to death. The survivors retreat to remote areas.

Food storage

The long, cold winter is the harshest time in temperate grasslands. Most small animals hibernate, waking sometimes to feed. Ground squirrels store grass seeds in their underground burrows. The Asian pika gathers together a haystack of grasses which it dries in the sun. It piles the hay into mounds weighing up to 20 pounds. In the winter, it lives cosily beneath its haystack, which is also its food supply.

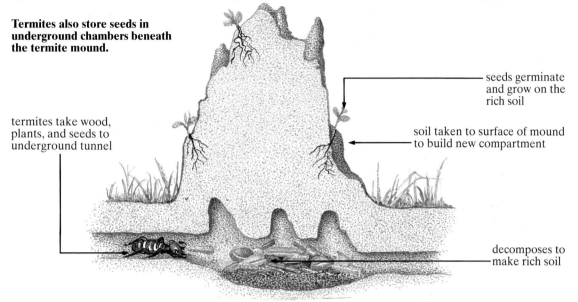

Termites also store seeds in underground chambers beneath the termite mound.

termites take wood, plants, and seeds to underground tunnel

seeds germinate and grow on the rich soil

soil taken to surface of mound to build new compartment

decomposes to make rich soil

Living together

In areas like the African savanna, the different kinds of animals must avoid competing for food. East Africa, especially, has large herds of buffalo, zebra, wildebeest, gazelle, and topi. In the wet season, there is enough short grass on the higher ground for all five species to feed. At the start of the dry season, this grass stops growing. The animals move to lower, wetter areas.

Buffalo, which eat large-leaved grasses growing along the river-banks, move first. Zebra, which eat the grass stems, follow them. Topi migrate to the northwest to feed on short mat-forming grasses. Wildebeest feed on the more upright grasses farther south and gazelles eat small broad-leaved plants uncovered by grass-grazers.

31

THREATENED GRASSLANDS

Many different grasslands of the world, for example reedbeds, are slowly disappearing. Freshwater reedbeds are food and shelter to a rich variety of wildlife. For thousands of years, people have harvested the reeds for thatching. Now, the largest and most valuable reedbeds are disappearing, as the land is drained and used for farming or building.

Temperate salt marshes are widespread but they do not cover a large area (see p. 24), so any loss is important. About a quarter of salt marshes in the U.S. and U.K. have been lost since the 1930s. Much, much more is at risk.

When salt marshes are drained, the land is suitable for horticulture, farming, or industrial uses, but such changes can drastically affect the remaining salt marsh. Fertilizers and sewage increase the phosphates and nitrates in the mud and this upsets the

Threats to savanna
Semidry savannas bordering deserts are at great risk from desertification. In places such as the Sahel region in Africa, changeable climate has meant years of drought. Herds of domestic goats have destroyed what little grass there was and the topsoil is being lost. Instead of dry grassland, it is turning into a desert. Cattle put to graze on savanna do not do as well as native herbivores which are used to the poor, coarse grasses. They are also more at risk from tropical diseases such as sleeping sickness.

balance of plants. Oil spills also kill salt marsh plants. Some recover quite quickly, but the salt marsh grass *Puccinellia* can take up to ten years to recover. Salt marsh turf is the natural grazing place for black brent goose, baldpate, and blue winged teal. If their feeding ground is reduced, hungry flocks of birds move onto farmland and eat cereal crops instead.

Threats to temperate grassland

Most of the prairies, steppes, pampas, and velds, the world's largest and most important temperate grasslands, have been plowed up. Instead of the once-rich variety of wild grasses and broad-leaved plants, there are now only wheatfields. Cereals are grown on about 70 percent of the world's crop lands and there is no room for wild native plants. Large animals are confined to national parks such as Yellowstone National Park, and Kruger National Park, South Africa. Small burrowing animals become pests and are controlled or killed.

Some grasslands are overgrazed by domestic animals, which damages the turf and exposes the soil. In Argentina, thorny, uneatable bushes have invaded the grassland. As there is no dry grass, fire cannot be used to control the thorn bushes. Either the grassland is lost, or money has to be spent in digging them up.

Australia and New Zealand

Rainfall is unpredictable over much of Australia. The two largest kangaroos, the red and the gray, travel long distances to patches of good grass. Their long hind feet are soft and do not damage the thin turf. When cattle and sheep were introduced, their hard hooves cut into the turf, adding to overgrazing problems.

Before Europeans settled in New Zealand, the plains of the South Island were tussocky grassland of fescues and meadow grasses. Seven species of introduced animals, together with domestic sheep, have completely altered the natural vegetation. Sometimes it has been destroyed and the topsoil lost.

GRAINS AND CEREALS

Over 10,000 years ago, in the fertile lands of the Middle East, people began to cultivate wheat. They chose two wild wheats, einkorn and emmer, as these had naturally large grains. As the growing population spread farther afield, they took their precious grains with them. Emmer, which cross-fertilized with a wild grass, produced a **hybrid**. Now called "bread wheat," it is one of the world's most important cereals. Since then many other grasses have been cultivated and used for flour, cereals, and food for livestock.

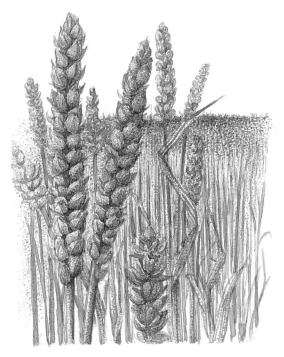

Wheat (*Triticum aestivum*)
Wheat is grown in warm, temperate climates. The best-quality wheat comes from the North American prairies and the steppes of the Soviet Union. It is also grown in Europe, South America, Asia, and Australia. Over 375 million tons are produced each year.

Wheat flour makes light bread because about 80 percent of its protein is sticky gluten. This traps the carbon dioxide gas given off by yeast, a microscopic fungus used to make dough rise.

Oats (*Avena sativa*)
Oats were originally a weed in early wheat and barley crops. It was first grown as a crop about 2,000 years ago. Both grain and straw are valuable food for domestic animals. It is very hardy and grows in cooler, damp climates with a short growing season. Most of it is used to feed livestock, especially horses, but it is also made into breakfast cereals. About 52 million tons a year are produced. Chief producers are North America, Europe, and the Soviet Union.

Barley (*Hordeum vulgare*)

Barley was also first cultivated about 10,000 years ago, in southwest Asia. It was made into bread and alcoholic drinks by many ancient peoples – the early Egyptians, Greeks, Chinese, and Japanese.

As it was planted farther north in Europe and Asia, people realized how hardy it was. It grew better than wheat on wetter, higher ground. It was cheaper than wheat, so barley bread was the daily fare of all but the wealthy until the sixteenth century. These flat, hard loaves are no longer made. Most barley grain is now used to feed livestock. The rest is brewed into beers and barley wine, or distilled into whisky. About 165 million tons of barley are produced each year. North America, Europe, the Soviet Union, and Asia are the leading producers.

Rye (*Secale cereale*)

Rye has been cultivated for about 2,000 years. Before this it was a weed in the wheat and barley crops and spread from southwest Asia to Europe. It is a hardy grass and grows well on poor, sandy, or acid soils where other cereals are not successful. It has long, stiff straw sometimes used for thatching. Although it does not have the high gluten content of wheat flour, rye flour is used to make dark bread in the Soviet Union, Poland, Germany, and Scandinavia. About 38 million tons of rye are produced each year. The chief producers are the Soviet Union, Poland, and West Germany.

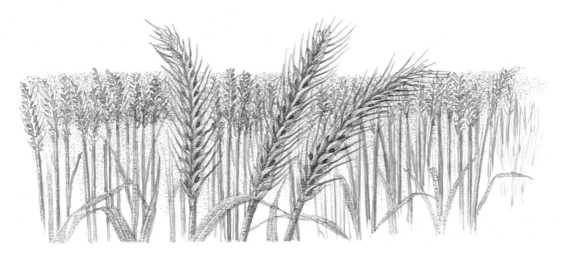

RICE AND SUGAR

About half the population of the world depends on rice. It was first cultivated about 5,500 years ago in Thailand and China, and soon after in India. Today, the chief rice-producing country is China, but most of the southeast Asian countries grow rice. It is well suited to these hot, wet monsoon countries, for unlike other cereals, rice needs waterlogged conditions.

Of the 440 million tons of rice produced each year, most is grown on small farms. The whole family helps with the rice crop, which has to feed them all through the year. Only the United States exports most of its crop.

All parts of the rice plant are used. The whole grain is cooked and eaten, the stems are woven into household goods, the bran is fed to chickens, and the broken grain is fermented into alcoholic drinks or ground into flour. Livestock feed on the stubble, or it is plowed into the soil.

Growing rice (*Oryza sativa*)

There are over 7,000 varieties of rice. Deep-water rice is grown in flooded river valleys in Thailand and Bangladesh. It has a long stem and the flowerheads float on the surface of the water. Harvesting is done by boat.

Swamp rice is grown in flooded fields called paddys (see below). The water is retained by low mud walls built around each field. About 90 percent of the world's rice is grown in this way.

Upland rice is grown on cool, wet hillsides. The many different kinds vary in size from 3 to 10 feet. The grain may be long or round, fluffy or sticky when cooked.

Sugar (*Saccharum officinarum*)

Sugarcane has been cultivated in southeast Asia for at least 3,000 years. Now grown in most tropical countries, about 650 million tons are produced each year, mainly by India.

Sugarcane grows quickly, reaching about 15 feet and may be 3 inches in diameter. The flowerheads are large panicles (see p. 19), but many canes do not flower. When seeds are formed, they are often infertile and cannot grow into new plants. However, sugarcane can be grown from cuttings.

To grow and get a good yield of sugary sap, this grass needs sunshine, water, and deep, fertile soil. The best stems are 85 percent juice, which contains about 20 percent sugars. Although sugarcane is harvested by machine in the U.S. and Australia, in most Asian countries it is still cut by hand. The cane is cut close to the ground. The tops of the stem and the leaves are not used. The cut canes are taken to the factories within 48 hours and made into various food and industrial products (see below).

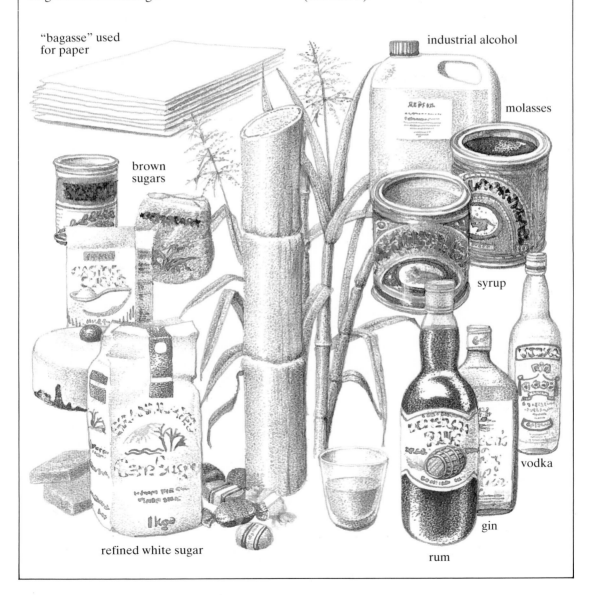

"bagasse" used for paper

industrial alcohol

molasses

brown sugars

syrup

vodka

gin

rum

refined white sugar

GRAIN FROM HOT CLIMATES

After wheat and rice, corn is the next most important cereal. It was first grown in Mexico nearly 5,000 years ago. Early Central American Indians bred many kinds, but no one knows what wild corn was like. Perhaps it was like teosinte, a small cornlike plant found today. Sorghum, millet, and teff are also grown in hot, dry climates.

Sorghum (*Sorghum bicolor*)
Sorghum is a tall, stiff grass grown in hot, tropical countries. It was first cultivated in Ethiopia between 5,000 and 6,000 years ago. From here it spread to other parts of tropical Africa, and across to India and China. Sorghum is drought resistant, and for many people in dry regions of the tropics, it is the staple food.

The grain is pounded into flour. It may also be fermented and made into beer, but neither flour nor beer will keep for very long. A sugary syrup can be squeezed from the stems of some kinds of sorghum.

Teff (*Eragrostis tef*)
Teff has been cultivated for thousands of years in Ethiopia. It is still grown in the Ethiopian highlands. Although its grain is tiny, less than $1/10$ inch long, teff is very valuable to the Ethiopians because it grows in conditions unsuitable for other cereals. The grains are ground into flour and made into large pancakes called "ingera."

Millets

Two of the most important millets are pearl millet (*Pennisetum americanum*) and finger millet (*Eleusine coracana*). Pearl millet is thought to be similar to the millets cultivated over 3,000 years ago in the Sahel region of West Africa. From there they were taken to East Africa and India.

Millets are very drought tolerant and will grow on drier, sandier soils than sorghum. This is important for the peoples of arid (very dry), hot lands. The grain is ground into flour and also fermented. Some millets can be stored for 10 years. This is a good precaution against famine.

China now produces most of the world's millets and sorghum. Over 110 million tons of these grains are produced each year.

Corn (*Zea mays*)

Corn is grown in warm parts of the world with a good rainfall and hot summers. It is a tall grass, with flowers arranged differently from other grasses. Male flowers are in tassels at the top of the stem. Female flowers grow lower down, in a cob wrapped in a leafy husk. Only the long silky styles are visible. When ripe, the grains are packed tightly around the cob. There are over 500 uses for corn. It provides food for livestock as well as for people. The flour cannot be made into bread, but the grain is used for breakfast cereals, cornmeal, starch, and cooking oil. About 350 million tons of corn are produced each year. The "corn belt" region of the United States produces almost half the world's corn.

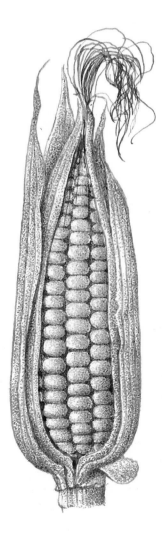

IMPROVING THE YIELD

The very first farmers did not have machines. They planted, weeded, harvested, and threshed the grain by hand. The early cereals were "grassier" than modern crops. The ripe ear was brittle, and shattered when touched. The grains were held tightly in papery bracts.

In the 1960s a new strain of wheat called Norin 10 was bred. It had dwarfing genes which meant it had shorter stems. Wheats with shorter stems and heavier ears were bred from this new cultivar. These "dwarf" wheats have been very successful in poor countries with large populations to feed, for example, India, Pakistan, and Mexico.

There are about 4.5 billion people in the world. This number increases year by year. At present, there is enough food produced to feed everyone, but many people are too poor to buy it. Food shortages are worst in the developing countries.

Breeding cereals

In the developed countries today, grain production is mechanized. The immense farms are often called "agribusinesses."

Agricultural researchers are continually breeding and testing new cultivars or strains of grain to try and increase yields. New cultivars have to conform to certain standards. They must give a high yield of good quality grain, which ripens quickly, and all at the same time. The ears must not shatter when ripe and the grain must not germinate in the ear or stack. The stems must be all the same height for mechanical harvesting, and they must not blow over in wind or rain. They must have a good resistance to fungal diseases and insect attack.

The Environmental Costs of Growing Grain

In a natural ecosystem (see p. 14), a variety of plants and animals live together as a community. However, farmers do not want a community, they only want to see the crop they have sown – wheat, corn, rice, or rye. When only one species is grown like this it is called a monoculture. Everybody needs good food to stay alive and healthy, but unfortunately, in the process of growing food for so many, the environment suffers.

■ For maximum yield, large amounts of artificial fertilizers are needed. Excess fertilizers drain into water supplies and rivers and pollute them, killing fish and other animals.

■ Vast areas of land all planted with the same crop often leads to an explosion in the numbers of pests, especially insects.

■ Chemical sprays used to control pests often leave harmful chemicals in the food we eat.

■ Chemical herbicides used to kill weeds often kill other plants. Many wild flowers are becoming rare or extinct.

■ Soil left bare after the crop is harvested and the land plowed leads to the erosion of topsoil. This can never be replaced.

OTHER USES OF GRASSES

As well as being the main source of food for the world, grasses have many other uses. Bamboos are very useful; their stems are woody and tough. The largest bamboos are used for building – houses, bridges, fences, and boats. In countries such as India, Burma, and China, they are used as scaffold poles. Bamboos are as valuable now as they were to people living centuries ago. Useful things made from bamboo include furniture, water pipes, farming and fishing equipment, household and kitchen utensils, masts, baskets, musical instruments, paper, weapons, ropes, brushes, and baskets.They even provide food as the shoots can be eaten.

Grasses for recreation grounds
Sports field turf has to be smooth, dense, and hard-wearing. Different mixtures of seeds are sown on carefully prepared ground. The mixture of seeds used depends on the kind of grass required. Seed for sports fields and recreational uses is grown commercially in Oregon and New Zealand.

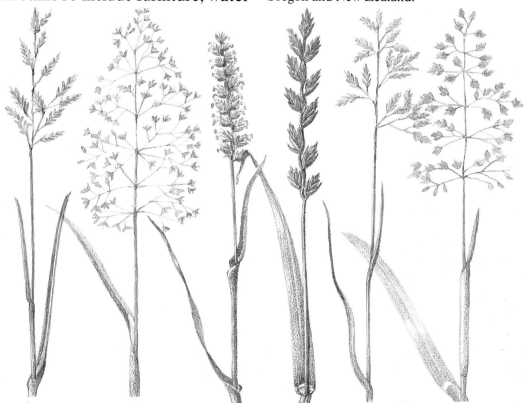

Chewing's fescue
(*Festuca rubra commutata*)

New Zealand browntop
(*Agrostis tenuis*)

crested dog's-tail
(*Cynosurus cristatus*)

perennial rye grass (*Lolium perenne*)

creeping red fescue
(*Festuca rubra*)

smooth stalked meadow grass
(*Poa pratensis*)

Weaving, plaiting, and thatching

Reeds and the tall stems of savanna grasses are often used to thatch roofs. Stems of many grasses all around the world are plaited and woven into hard-wearing mats and containers.

Grasses for perfumes

A group of grasses growing in tropical Africa and India contain fragrant oils. These oils are used in perfumes and cosmetics. The leaves are also used for teas and local medicines.

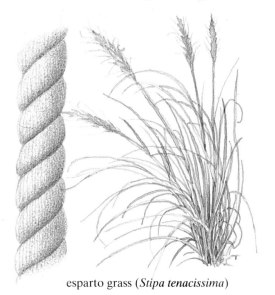

esparto grass (*Stipa tenacissima*)

vetiver (*Vetiveria zizanoides*) is used to make perfume

Brewing

Most grains are fermented into alcoholic beers, but beer made from barley is the most commercially important. This beer is made from germinated barley grain, called malt. The malt is dried and mixed with yeast. As the yeast grows, it produces alcohol. Dried hop flowers from the hop plant *Humulus lupulus* are added to give it the characteristically bitter taste. The U.S., West Germany, and the U.K. produce the most beer.

Grain	Beer	Distilled spirit	Where produced
Barley	Beers, Lagers, Stouts		U.S., West Germany, U.K.
		Whisky	Scotland
Corn		Bourbon, Whisky	U.S.
	Chicha		Central America and Andes
Proso millet	Beer		India, Africa
Rice	Sake		Japan, China
Rye		Gin	Netherlands
		Aquavit	Denmark
Sorghum	Beer		East, Central, and South Africa

GLOSSARY

ANGIOSPERMS – Flower plants with seeds that develop inside a fruit.

ANTHER – The part of a stamen that contains pollen grains.

AWN – A thin bristle on the glumes or lemmas of some grass flowers.

BLADE – The upper part of each grass leaf. It bends away from the stem at a node.

CARPEL – The female part of the flower made up of a stigma, style, and ovary.

CARYOPSIS – The grass fruit, consisting of a single seed and the very thin fruit wall.

CHLOROPHYLL – The green pigment that uses energy in sunlight to convert carbon dioxide and water into sugars.

CROSS-FERTILIZATION – This occurs when the pollen containing the fertilizing male cell comes from a different plant from the ovule.

CROSS-POLLINATION – This occurs when pollen from one plant pollinates a flower on a different plant.

DICOTYLEDONS – Plants that produce two seed-leaves, or cotyledons.

DORMANCY – The interval between seed ripening and germination.

EMBRYO – The part of a seed that grows into a new plant.

ENDOSPERM – The food-store of a seed.

EVAPORATION – Water lost to the air as water vapor.

FERTILIZATION – The entry and joining of a male pollen cell with the female ovule.

FILAMENT – A thin stalk that supports the pollen sac, or anther.

FRUIT – The part of a flower that contains and protects the developing seed or seeds.

GERMINATION – This is when a seed swells, sprouts, and starts to grow into a new plant.

GLUMES – Two small, leafy scales at the base of each flower spikelet.

HYBRID – A plant that is the result of flowers of two different species cross-pollinating.

INTERNODE – The length of grass stem between two nodes.

LEMMA – The lower of two scales enclosing each grass flower.

LODICULES – Two very tiny scales in the grass flower.

MONOCOTYLEDONS – Plants that have only one seed-leaf, or cotyledon.

NODE – The part of a grass stem where the leaf sheath is attached.

ORGANISM – Any living thing – plant, animal, bacterium, fungus.

OVARY – The part of the flower that contains the ovule.

OVULE – The female "cell" that grows into a seed after fertilization.

PALEA – The upper of two small scales enclosing each grass flower.

PANICLE – A spreading, branched flowerhead.

PHOTOSYNTHESIS – The process in green plants that turns carbon dioxide and water into sugars, using the energy in sunlight and releasing oxygen.

PISTIL – The whole of the female part of the flower which in grasses is made up of one carpel.

POLLEN GRAIN – A male "cell" that after pollination fertilizes an ovule.

RHIZOME – A creeping underground stem that can produce new plants at the nodes.

SEED – The fully developed, fertilized ovule. It contains an embryo and a food-store, and can grow into a new plant.

SELF-FERTILIZATION – This occurs when a male cell comes from pollen of the same plant as the ovule.

SELF-POLLINATION – This occurs when pollen from one plant pollinates a flower on the same plant.

SPIKE – A narrow, unbranched flowerhead.

STAMEN – The male part of the flower.

STIGMA – The part of the carpel upon which pollen lands.

STOLON – A stem that creeps along the surface of the ground, new plants growing at the nodes.

STYLE – The stem that supports the stigma.

TESTA – The outermost layer, or skin, of a seed.

GRASSES IN THIS BOOK

Andropogon species
Bamboo (*Melocanna* species)
Bamboo (*Sinarundinaria* species)
Barley (*Hordeum vulgare*)
Bermuda grass (*Cynodon dactylon*)
Big bluestem (*Andropogon gerardii*)
Brachiaria decumbens
Brachiaria dictyonema
Brachiaria humidicola
Breadwheat (*Triticum aestivum*)
Buffalo grass (*Buchloe dactyloides*)
Chee grass (*Stipa splendens*)
Chewing's fescue (*Festuca rubra* var *commutata*)
Chloris pycnothrix
Cocksfoot (*Dactylis glomerata*)
Common cord grass (*Spartina anglica*)
Common reed (*Phragmites australis*)
Common salt marsh grass (*Puccinellia maritima*)
Corn (*Zea mays*)
Couch grass (*Agropyron repens*)
Creeping red fescue (*Festuca rubra*)
Crested dog's-tail (*Cynosurus cristatus*)
Cymbopogon
Einkorn (*Triticum boeoticum*)
Elephant grass (*Pennisetum purpureum*)
Emmer (*Triticum dicoccoides*)
Esparto grass (*Stipa tenacissima*)
Feather grass (*Stipa pennata*)
Fescues (*Festuca* species)
Finger millet (*Eleusine coracana*)
Giant bamboo (*Dendrocalamus giganteus*)
Hare's-tail (*Lagurus ovatus*)
Hyparrhenia

Indian grass (*Sorghastrum nutans*)
Marram grass (*Ammophila arenaria, Ammophila* species)
Meadow grass (*Poa pratensis*)
Mitchell grasses (*Astrebla* species)
Needlegrasses (*Stipa* species)
New Zealand browntop (*Agrostis tenuis*)
Oats (*Avena sativa*)
Pampas grass (*Cortaderia selloana*)
Pearl millet (*Pennisetum americanum*)
Perennial rye-grass (*Lolium perenne*)
Proso millet (*Panicum miliaceum*)
Red fescue (*Festuca rubra* var. *arenaria*)
Reed (*Phragmites* species)
Rice (*Oryza sativa*)
Rooigrass or Red oats grass (*Themeda triandra*)
Rye (*Secale cereale*)
Small cordgrass (*Spartina maritima*)
Smooth cordgrass (*Spartina alternifolia*)
Sorghum (*Sorghum bicolor*)
Spinifex grasses (*Triodia* species)
Sporobolus marginatus
Sugarcane (*Saccharum officinarum*)
Switchgrass (*Panicum virgatum*)
Teff (*Eragrostis tef*)
Teosinte (*Zea mexicana*)
Timothy grass (*Phleum pratense*)
Totter or Common quaking grass (*Briza media*)
Uva grass (*Gynerium sagittatum*)
Vetiver (*Vetiveria zizanoides*)
Viviparous fescue (*Festuca vivipara*)
Wavy hair-grass (*Deschampsia flexuosa*)
Wheat (*Triticum aestivum*)
Wheatgrass (*Agropyron smithii*)

FURTHER READING

For children:

Cereals by Jacqueline Dineen; Enslow Publishers, 1988.
Living in Grasslands by Leo Robert; Watts, 1988.
Rice by Sylvia A. Johnson; Lerner Publications, 1985.
Sugar by Jacqueline Dineen; Enslow Publishers, 1988.

For adults:

Field Guide to the Grasses, Sedges & Rushes of the United States; Dover, 1977.
Grasses: An Identification Guide by Lauren Brown; Peterson Native Library, 1979.
Ornamental Grasses by Peter Loewer; Brooklyn Botanic, 1989.
Wheat, Millet & Other Grains by Beatrice T. Hunter; Keats, 1982.

INDEX

L
Lagurus ovatus 8
lemma 18, 19, 21
lodicules 18, 19
Lolium perenne 29, 42

M
marram grasses 26-27
meadow grasses 12, 23, 33, 42
Melocanna bamboo 21
Mexico 38, 40
migration 15, 30
millet 15, 30, 38, 39
Mitchell grasses 15
monocotyledons 6, 8, 9
monoculture 41
monsoon 17, 36

N
needlegrasses 13
New Zealand 29, 33, 42
New Zealand browntop 42
Norin 10 40
nutrients 11, 15, 26, 30

O
oats 12, 34
organisms 15
Oryza sativa 36
ovary 18, 19, 20, 21
ovules 8, 18, 20

P
Pakistan 40
palea 18, 21
pampas 6, 14, 33
panicle 18, 19, 37
paspalum 15
pasture 28, 29
pearl millet 39
Pennisetum species 16, 39
perennial rye-grass 23, 29, 42
perfumes 43
Phleum pratense 29
photosynthesis 9, 22
Phragmites reeds 24
plains 12, 14, 30
Poa pratensis 12, 42
pollen 8, 18, 20

pollination 20
prairies 12, 30, 33, 34
pronghorn antelope 13
proso millet 43
Puccinellia maritima 24, 32

R
rainfall 10, 11, 12, 14, 17, 27, 33
red fescue 27
reedbeds 24, 25, 30, 32
rhizomes 23, 25, 27
rice 36, 38, 43
rooigrass 16
roots 8, 9, 18, 19, 22, 25, 26
rye 12, 29, 35, 43

S
Saccharum officinarium 37
salt marshes 24, 32
sand dunes 26-27
savanna 7, 10-11, 16-17, 28, 30, 31, 32
Secale cereale 35
seeds 6, 8, 20-21, 22, 30-31
sheath 6, 22
sheep 12, 14, 15, 28, 33
Sinarundinaria bamboo 17
slacks 27
small cord grass 25
smooth cord grass 25
soil 9, 11, 15, 29, 41
sorghum 30, 38, 39, 43
Sorghum bicolor 38
South America 7, 10, 14, 16, 17, 29, 34
Soviet Union 7, 12, 34, 35
Spartina alternifolia 25
Spartina anglica 25
Spartina maritima 25
spikelets 6, 18, 19, 21, 23
spinifex 6, 27
Sporobolus marginatus 16
sports field turf 42
stamen 18, 19
stem 18, 21, 22, 23
steppes 12, 30, 33, 34
stigma 18, 19, 20
Stipa pennata 12
Stipa splendens 12

stolon 23
sugar 37
switchgrass 13

T
teff 6, 38
temperate grassland 7, 10-11, 12-15, 29, 31, 33
teosinte 38
termites 30, 31
testa 20, 21
thatching 24, 32, 35, 43
Themeda triandra 16
timothy grass 29
Triodia species 27
Triticum aestivum 34
tropical grasses 6

U
U.K. 25, 29, 43
U.S. 7, 12, 25, 30, 32, 33, 34, 35, 36, 37, 39, 43
uva grass 14

V
velds 14, 33
vetiver 43
Vetiver zizanoides 43
viviparous fescue 23

W
wavy hair grass 8
West Indies 16
wheat 12, 14, 21, 33, 34-35, 38, 40
wheatgrass 13
white clover 29
wildebeest 16, 31

X
xerophytes 26

Y
yeast 34, 43
Yellowstone National Park 33

Z
Zea mays 39
zebra 16, 31
zones 7, 10-11